the milestones
project

the milestones project

CELEBRATING CHILDHOOD AROUND THE WORLD

PHOTOGRAPHY BY Dr. Richard Steckel and Michele Steckel

Tricycle Press
Berkeley | Toronto

To Taylor Ryan, Conor Ryan, Aidan Loughran,

Sutton Loughran, Maddie Sanders, Josh Sanders, and Max DeWan—

our cherished grandchildren and future peacemakers.

—R. S. and M. S.

ACKNOWLEDGMENTS

Continuing and heart-felt thanks to Wayne and Jody
Rigsby (www.artfarmdesign.com), Brian Payne
(www.brianpayne.com), Jim and Kathy Armstrong
(www.goodforbusiness.com), Jenny Lehman, Robin
Simons, John Imbergamo, and Bruce Hutton.

Tricycle Press
a little division of Ten Speed Press
P.O. Box 7123
Berkeley, California 94707
www.tenspeed.com

Tax-deductible donations can be sent to
The Milestones Project Fund at the Denver Foundation
5443 South Prince Street, Littleton, Colorado 80120
(303) 572-3333, or online at www.milestonesproject.com.

Design by Catherine Jacobes Design
Typeset in Syntax, Chaparral, and Clarendon

Library of Congress Cataloging-in-Publication Data on file
ISBN-10: 1-58246-132-5
ISBN-13: 978-158246-132-8

First Tricycle Press printing, 2004
Printed in Singapore

2 3 4 5 6 7 — 09 08 07 06 05

Editor's Note: Throughout the text original spellings and sentence
structure have been retained, most visibly in contributions from children.

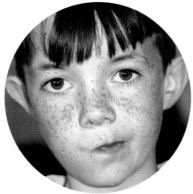

contents

We do not remember days,

we remember moments.

—Anonymous

introduction

Why We Created this Book

The Milestones Project began with a single camera and is, at the time of this writing, an ever-growing archive of 23,000 photographs. Many wonderful photographs, more than can appear in a single book, can be found at www.milestonesproject.com. Those who have joined us in the Project share a sense of awe in those moments when a child is engaged in an experience common to children everywhere. It is truly inspiring to see a milestone reached.

This is the essence of The Milestones Project, a comprehensive effort to document childhood experiences in places far and wide. We aim to create a more peaceful world by encouraging the recognition that, beneath our beliefs or skin color, we are all the same; we are a single people, striving for joy and meaning in an unpredictable world. When children from every continent, from different races and

"I do studies about young people and how they see the world they live in. In one study, I asked kids in the third through twelfth grades from all over the U.S. what they would remember the most from this particular period in their lives. I also asked their parents to guess what their children would say. The parents tended to guess the big events—the special parties or trips.

"But that's not what kids said. They mentioned the small everyday moments—the song their mother sings to them in the morning when they wake up, the walks on Saturdays with their father, the special time they have reading with a grandparent.

"I have shared this finding with so many fathers and mothers, and it has helped them know to make the small everyday moments with their children more special."

—Ellen Galinsky
author and president and co-founder of Families and Work Institute

traditions, different countries and cultures, see something of themselves in one another, they know deep inside that they are part of a universal family. This book strives to diminish hatred by alleviating fear, one young person at a time. Looking at these photographs should help rid our world of the ignorance that says, "they are different from me so I cannot trust them."

What a Milestone Means to Us

To understand each other, it's important to remember that we all reach the same milestones as we grow from baby to child to teenager to grown-up. Here are the turning points of childhood, marvelously captured in words and photographs. The more stories read and the more pictures seen, the less fear we have of people who look, talk, or act differently than we do. These pictures remind us of all we share with people in every country on earth. And this is a first step toward creating the peace we long for.

"Be nice and care. Be nice to others, or bad luck will come your way."
—Jack, age 5, USA

What Children Get from this Book

Kids love looking at photographs of themselves. "That's me!" they shout. They get almost as much pleasure looking at pictures of other children. But their experience is more than that. When the image shows a situation they know themselves, children have an amazing capacity to empathize, to virtually become the child in the photograph and recognize what they have in common rather than what sets them apart.

Ellen Galinsky, president and co-founder of Families and Work Institute, conducts studies about young people and how they see the world. In one study, she asked kids all over the United States, "If you had one wish to stop the violence that you experience today, what would that wish be?" The largest group of kids (in the fifth through the twelfth grades) wanted to stop the teasing, bullying, and rejecting they were all familiar with. They wrote that kids pick on kids who look different. Most of the time, they don't want to tease others, but they feel afraid that if they don't join in, they will be ridiculed themselves. It is the small things that lead to the big problems. . . and big solutions.

"To change the world we must begin with children. This is as true for ending poverty as it is for ending the stereotypes that fuel hatred and violence. As the world searches for solutions to seemingly intractable problems, let's draw on the inherent strengths of children. With their openness, selflessness, good sense, creativity, and unspoiled faith in the possibilities of life, they can certainly teach us much about ending the fears and stereotypes that divide us.

"Two children stood before the United Nations General Assembly... and explained that a world fit for children is a world fit for everyone. It is one from which the evils of discrimination have been purged, one in which all people 'treat each other with dignity and respect' and are 'open and sensitive to our differences.' No one can really say it better than that.

"Discrimination hurts everyone, those who discriminate and those discriminated against."

—Carol Bellamy,
executive director of UNICEF

"Racism, racial discrimination, xenophobia, and all kinds of related intolerance…persist in the new century and their persistence is rooted in fear: fear of what is different, fear of the other, fear of the loss of personal security.

"We all constitute one human family. This truth has now become self-evident because of the first mapping of the human genome, an extraordinary achievement which not only reaffirms our common humanity but promises transformations in…the visions which our species can entertain for itself…. And it could make the twenty-first century an era of genuine fulfillment and peace.

"The horrors of racism…are still with us in various forms. It is now time to confront them and to take comprehensive measures against them."

—the Honorable Mary Robinson,
former president of Ireland and United Nations high commissioner for human rights

Kids can make a really big splash in the world, like jumping into a calm lake and making not just ripples but real waves. There are thousands of kids who have seen something they wanted to change—in their communities, in their schools, in their environment—and they started talking to their friends about it. And those friends talked to their friends. Some of the grown ups around them started to notice what these kids were saying. And together, they made change happen.

"I need a year to stop hatred. First, at my own country. After, I try by going to each country, talk to people province by province, and hear their problems and why they hate another people…. I can stop hatred by communication."
—Gracious, age 9, South Africa

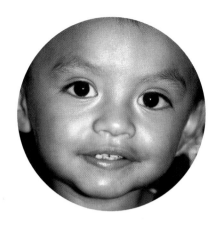

"If everyone started sharing with each other and people started playing with each other and doing favors for each other, I think the whole world would be happy."
—Brooklyn, age 7, USA

There is one simple way to make a difference: Share this book with others. Share it with friends and laugh together at the photographs of kids doing what kids do. Share it with grown-ups—neighbors, aunts, uncles, grandparents. Ask these adults if they remember the milestones in their own lives. Share it with schoolmates and teachers. Talk about the milestones together. Invite others to listen to your discussion.

Then, take The Milestones Project pledge on page 64. Because that is how the world changes. One person at a time.

Enjoy the original writings created specifically for this book. We have chosen to retain the spellings and punctuation of the children's pieces to preserve the voice behind their words.

"As a society, we can make our world a better place. We must all roll up our sleeves and work individually and collectively to make this planet more livable. We owe it to ourselves. We owe it to our children. We owe it to humanity."
—The Honorable Joseph Clark,
former prime minister of Canada

—Dr. Richard Steckel and Michele Steckel

Producers, The Milestones Project

birthdays

Something special in my life was when I was sleeping all my family was there with a cake and they put a CD with the birthday song "Las Mañanitas." They really gave me a surprise and I woke up very happy. And that dream came true.

—Jonny, age 10, Venezuela

Philippines

My cake just had a red and blue car on it. The red one got lost. I was just 5. I was good when I was three 3 kids came and there parent too. The toys on top of my cake were my present.

—Tlaloc, age 6, USA

New Zealand

My favorite birthday was when I was little, but I don't remember which year.

—Yoni, age 10, Guatemala

South Afr

12

Every Day Is a Milestone

When I was a child, every day was a milestone. Holidays, dramatic days, meant less to me than the common days passing like the breeze. I wanted time to stop. I wanted to be held in every moment. On my third birthday I cried because I did not feel finished with two.

And when I was eight, my father and I had our photos taken together in a little photo booth in a store somewhere in St. Louis. I had never heard of such a magical thing before—put in a quarter and in a few moments your pictures come popping out.

—Naomi Shihab Nye

On my fifth birthday, 7 August 1941, we had a family photograph taken. My younger sisters Joan and Heather were unsure of the man who kept putting his head under a black cloth to take our picture. The flashgun he held high in one hand sputtered light and smoke like the bombs we saw on movie newsreels. World War II was not in New Zealand, but it crouched around us, and we felt its threat in blackouts, rationing, barbed wire on the beaches, the grey photos of servicemen killed or missing in action. In our family portrait, my father wore a badge that told people he had volunteered for service but had been turned down for health reasons. He hid his anxiety from us. "This is a war to end all wars," he told us. "When this is over, there will never be a war again."

—Joy Cowley

I had my very
first birthday I was 1.
I had to put my face in the
cake. It was very gud. My
fass was very dirdy.

—Seande, age 7, USA

USA

Canada

My 6th birthday party was so grat.
We played pin the dot on the ladybug!
We ate spaghetti and we played a game
called. Well we played a game! And it
went like this…a person was supposed
to chase us and we had to find a mom
and we had to find a baby. And it was
so fun! And it was a slumber party and
at night we got to stay up late at
night. And boys were not allowd.

—Saqera-Maat, age 6, USA

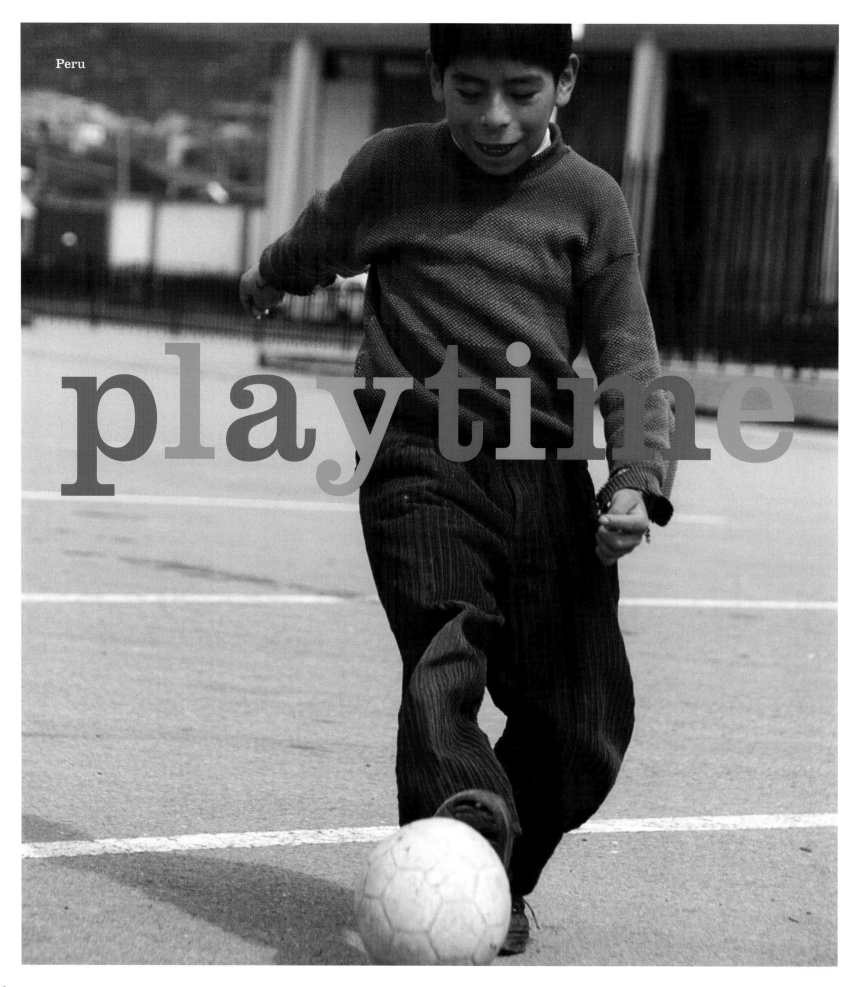

Peru

playtime

My first time off training weels is when I was about 4 years old and I kept on trying and trying to get it but I couldn't get it but a week latter my mom pushed me and I rode my bike down the steps and I got it finly. I was so excited! I rode it every day and the next day and I got better and better. And that's how I learned how to ride my bike! The end.

—Cassidy, age 8, USA

New Zealand

When I wus 3
I got a bear that
wus 3 feet log.

—Gaia, age 6, USA

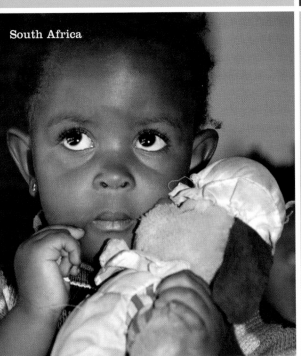

My first toy
was Bunny. I still take
Bunny to bed now
that I am older.

—Stephanie, age 9, New Zealand

My favorite toy is
a doll without hair!
And also I love the
little dishes for
pretend cooking.

—Astrid, age 8, Guatemala

My Favorite Toy—Punky Bear

Everyone has a teddy bear from their early years—I had a very normal looking one that was called Teddy; I had it since I was born. In 1977, when I was thirteen, I got into punk music. There was always a bit of competition between punks and teddy boys, so I decided I couldn't own a teddy bear and that he would have to become Punky Bear. Over the course of the summer, he obtained a shaved Mohican, dyed green hair, an assortment of safety pins attached to different parts of him, and generally a very scruffy appearance. As I started to learn to play guitar and was in bands, Punky too was provided with a number of cardboard guitars complete with boxes as amplifiers. He even appeared in one of our gigs sitting on my amp.

Unfortunately for Punky, as I moved through the '80s and '90s getting into new and different types of music, he remained and still is today, a rather sad and unfashionable bear.

—**Stephen Pankhurst**

The Playhouse

I grew up with four big sisters. My ironworker dad built us a playhouse—a pint-sized, barn-red replica of our own brick house, complete with glass-paned windows and a porch with awnings. I'll never forget the day he wheeled the whole thing out into the driveway...on roller skates! We made our mark, pressing our handprints into the newly cemented sidewalk leading up to the front door.

The playhouse was magical to me, the first real place to call my own. It was here that I had my first tea parties and sleepovers; here that we made up the games of Restaurant and Lady. By day, I imagined myself Laura Ingalls Wilder in her log cabin; by night, Anne Frank hiding out in her attic.

Over the years, my sisters and I left home one by one. The porch began sagging, the awnings faded. For years, that playhouse was just a spidery home to rakes and shovels. After the death of my parents, the new owners had only one request: tear down that unsightly "outbuilding." My playhouse. On the final weekend before the sale of the house, in below-freezing Pennsylvania temperatures, I stood solemnly facing the playhouse, my husband Richard and my cousin Jimmy at my side, crowbars in hand. In no time, my playhouse became a scrap heap of splintered wood, fallen shingles, and loose nails.

I saved one of those old square-headed nails. It sits on my desk, next to a jar of pencils. In that nail is a handful of childhoods, a hundred stories. In that nail is a whole heaven of memories, the place from which I write.

—**Megan McDonald**

In 1967 I realized that the only way I could eat English peas without suffering a violent physical reaction was to pretend I was from another planet and that the small green orbs were the greatest of all my planet's culinary delicacies. While eating these intergalactic wonders I would wear appropriate dining gear and make loud, disgusting sounds as was the custom of my new native planet. Eventually my father paid me 75 cents to stop this alien behavior. This episode began a pattern that would eventually consume my adult life. If reality is not working out I make up an alternative that suits me and get paid for it.

—**William Joyce**

India

My favorite toy is my dancing spinning top,
and the Transformer and an airplane and a remote
control boat that the cat can really ride in.

—Fernando, age 5, Venezuela

New Zealand

USA

New Zealand

Every child likes to play with friends. I was a playful child. I loved to skip and run, and tumble and chase, and call and scream with friends and all. Best of all, I simply loved to play by moonlight when a full moon sashayed low in the sky and every child came out to the sandy village square to frolic in the silver light.

MOONLIGHT PLAY
We played upon the silver sands,
Glistening by the light of the moon;
Feet in air, we stood on our hands
Till we came tumbling down quite soon.

We sang old songs—some sad, some sweet,
And followed the fireflies everywhere;
We clapped our hands, we tapped our feet,
We frolicked in the warm night air.

At last, upon the sand we lay
And listened to tales of Tortoise and Hare;
The night was still as bright as day
When we slept off without a care.

—Uzo Unobagha

When I was only five years old, on Christmas, the "Niño Jesus" (baby Jesus is the one that brings the presents in Venezuela) brought me three toys—one little wooden horse, very simple with some wheels on its legs, and two other toys that I don't remember. The thing is that when I saw that little horse I felt so fascinated that I didn't pay any attention to the other two gifts. My family couldn't understand what qualities this little horse had. It was the cheapest, most modest of all presents. According to them the other two toys were in fashion, more expensive, maybe even more sophisticated. But, I fell in love with my little wooden horse because I could roll it and make it my companion, imagining that it galloped, jumped, and participated in circuses. From that moment on I felt a special fascination for horses. With that experience I understood that happiness could come out of simple things, that imagination can make out of toys what no mechanism can, make a horse fly, swim, or transform it into a hero or friend.

—Oscar Misle

lost teeth

Philippines

South Africa

USA

I thought it was neat when my brother and sister lost their first teeth. When I lost my first tooth, everybody in my family was very proud of me. My daddy said, "I am very proud of you." It was night time when I lost my first tooth. I wiggled it all day before my dad pulled it out, and it felt FUNNY! Mom said I was the youngest kid in our family to lose a tooth. I loved losing my first tooth, because the Tooth Fairy gave me 2 dollars. I have my very own Tooth Fairy, her name is Angel and I love her.

—Aidan, age 7, USA

My Lost Tooth

That tooth, right in the front, had been wobbling and wobbling for weeks. I liked it wobbling. When I had nothing else to do or when I wanted to make someone laugh—or scare them off!—I'd open my mouth and wobble that tooth with my tongue. But one morning I woke up and the wobbly tooth was gone. My brother said a fairy had taken it and would leave me a present in return. Well, he could be right because, the next morning, on my bedside table, I found a shiny bright silver coin.

After that, I had more wobbly teeth. I know what happened to them. I pulled them out so they wouldn't get lost. But a mystery remains: What happened to that first wobbly tooth? If indeed a fairy took it— what did they want it for, I wonder.

—**Kara May**

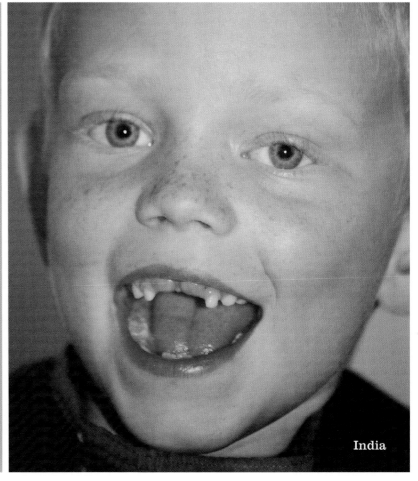

India

Kenya

When I lost my first tooth, I swallowed it at school during lunch. We had been waiting so long for this loose tooth to come out.

—Stephanie, age 9, New Zealand

Malaysia

My first tooth was lost. I pulled my tooth out my mom help me. I got twenty five cents under my pillow. I bought lots of candy.

—Desmond, age 6, USA

New Zealand

When I lost my first tooth I felt very happy and it didn't hurt at all. After it hurt a lot. And time goes by and it doesn't hurt at all.

—Maria, age 9, Venezuela

Sri Lanka

My friend Aryaman came to the park with me. First we played a bit then I ran up a slide and at the top there was a big bar. I wasn't looking where I was going so I hit my tooth on it and it was half out so I went down to my nanny Nina and she pulled it out. And that was when my first tooth fell out.

—Joseph, age 8, United Kingdom

St. Lucia

26

Ireland

My First tooth fell out when I was 6. I was glad to have a wiggly
tooth, and ate lots of apples hoping for it to come lose. I pulled it
out when I was in bed one night. I was excited about the tooth fairy
coming, She forgot the first night. The next night she remembered,
though and she left a $1.00. I was very glad.

—Liam, age 8, New Zealand

friends

Peru

I don't have a best friend,
all of my friends are good.

—Yoni, age 10, Guatemala

Siblings

I grew up with three sisters in an old house in the middle of Chicago. As a special treat our grandmother once took us downtown to see prima ballerina Margot Fontaine dance in *Swan Lake*. We were absolutely spellbound by the exquisite dancing, and of course, we wanted to be ballerinas too! When we got home there were no tiaras or sparkling tutus, but that didn't stop our imaginations for a moment. We simply dressed up and invented our own romantic ballets where we could leap, twirl, and be beautiful tragic heroines like Margot Fontaine. The power of make-believe is truly magical—how else do faded old scarves turn into dazzling costumes, gym socks become pink satin ballet slippers, and four stocky little girls transform into graceful swans?

—Katharine Holabird

Slovakia

Special Friend

Me and my buddy M had so much fun, the kind of fun you have with a newly found friend when everything in life is open and unexplored. I knew somewhere deep inside we were different, but I didn't know how and I really didn't have time to find out. We met every day and fooled around. One time he took me to the apartment where his family lived. I remember how uncomfortable I felt there. Everything was worn down, ugly—not at all like where I lived. I also felt guilty for having these thoughts. I was kind of shocked when he told me he didn't have a room of his own. He slept in a sofa. He didn't have books, games, or toys. I mean, no toys! In a drawer, he showed me a knife which was his. That's when I realised how we were unalike. Not all kids have toys. Many kids are poor, don't have toothbrushes, never see doctors, never ever get to go to school. His world was different from mine no matter how much crazy fun we had in the world we shared.

—**Daniel Möller**

Siblings

I was the oldest of a family of five. I remember the various mysterious appearances of three sisters and a brother. My mother would vanish from the family home for a while—over ten days back in the past. On the first occasion, I was not really told why she had gone. I simply stayed with my uncle and aunt and my cousin and had a good time. But then my mother came home with a baby. I was filled with happy excitement. Everything was amazing...the delicate newness of the baby itself...the mystery of seeing it get milk from my mother's breast...the drama of its dirty napkins and the subsequent lines of washing (for of course these were in the days before disposable naps).

I can remember looking at the babies with unconditional love and pleasure, and I can remember the excitement when we had a boy baby in the family. His first bath was dramatic in a new way. My sisters and I studied his small male organs with fascination, and with satisfaction too, partly because we were pleased to have a brother at last and perhaps because a basic human difference of which we were aware—but which was hugely masked by the perceptions of the time— had become a little more distinct to us. As the babies grew and became children, we inevitably had the arguments and fights that tend to dominate family life, but I remember...I will always remember... those first wonderful confrontations. My sisters and brother cannot remember me as a baby, but I can remember every one of them. They were all special, and though we now live such separate lives, we are still tied into one another in marvelous ways and have been from our very first meetings.

—**Margaret Mahy**

St. Lucia

New Zealand

When I was 4 and in my second school I made a friend named Yanis. (Sometimes I call her YaYa.) but it took a while for her to know me but we became friends and now we are best friends. We've gotten to have another best friend her name is Tatiana and I have been friends for 4 years and I really love my friends.

—Vanessa, age 8 3/4, USA

I was born with my two first friends we grew up together. We wood go down town to ride bikes, skatbords and scooters.

—Dillon, age 9, USA

Philippin

Bianca is my best friend.
We play together all the time and
I always have to go over to her house
all the time and I call her to but the
only thing I don't do with her is
we don't have rules.

—Gabriela, age 7, USA

When I herd Eliza was born
I was so happy that I cryd. I was
suprisd that Eliza was so small. When
she was 1 she came up to my bed and
she took my bear and now it is her
favorit bear. Eliza is very anoying but
she is my favorit sister. Sometimes
when Eliza crys I cry too.

—Chloe, age 7, USA

Sri Lanka

My first friend her name was Savanha. We were best friends sence we were babies. I am one year older than her. She lives in Alpine and I live here so it's just a short drive away. But now we don't ever get to see each other anymore. But we are still friends in our hearts.

—Elizabeth, age 8, USA

Twice in my life, before I was even eight years old, I had to learn a language different from my native tongue. Born in Puerto Rico, my family and I spoke only Spanish. At the age of four, I began the traveling life of an "army brat," as my family moved to Missouri, then to France, and finally to California. Like most kids, I wanted very much to have friends. But to do that I had to learn their language. In Missouri, my first friends spoke a strange language that sounded like gobbledygook. I tried to imitate what they said by making up nonsense words that sounded like theirs. They, in turn, imitated what I had said. We spent the first day speaking gobbledygook to one another, thinking that we were speaking one another's language. But by the time I started kindergarten, I spoke English as well as my friends.

When I started third grade, we moved to France. My mom insisted that we live in town and experience the French culture. A few months later, my mom noticed that I was unhappy because I still had no friends. She had already learned a little French, so she asked the landlady's daughter if she would play with me. Of course, I was embarrassed that my "mami" was doing what I should have done myself. But it all worked out, and Martine became my best friend. She spoke absolutely no English. But being a clever girl, Martine used a blackboard to teach me the conjugation of verbs, the way she learned in school. Within a few months, I spoke perfect French.

—**Marisa Montes**

Siblings

I was born on my brother's second birthday. We were always best friends, and our lives revolved around our books. We loved to read adventure stories and then pretend that we were the characters in the books. With our many friends, we would run around our Berkeley neighborhood dressed up as pirates in *Treasure Island* or as Indians in *The Last of the Mohicans*. It was a magical time. But what I remember best was when my brother spent one summer writing a science fiction novel of his own. Although he was only eight years old, he was determined to finish it before summer vacation ended. At night, in the little attic bedroom we shared, he would read to me what he had written during the day. Although his novel was never published, I remember how exciting it was that summer, thinking that my brother was going to be a famous author, just like Jack London.

—Daniel San Souci

Canada

Ireland

I remember the day my brother was born. He came home from the hospital. I thot he was a puppy. I asked if we cood keep him. I was 18 munths old.

—Jordan, age 7, USA

35

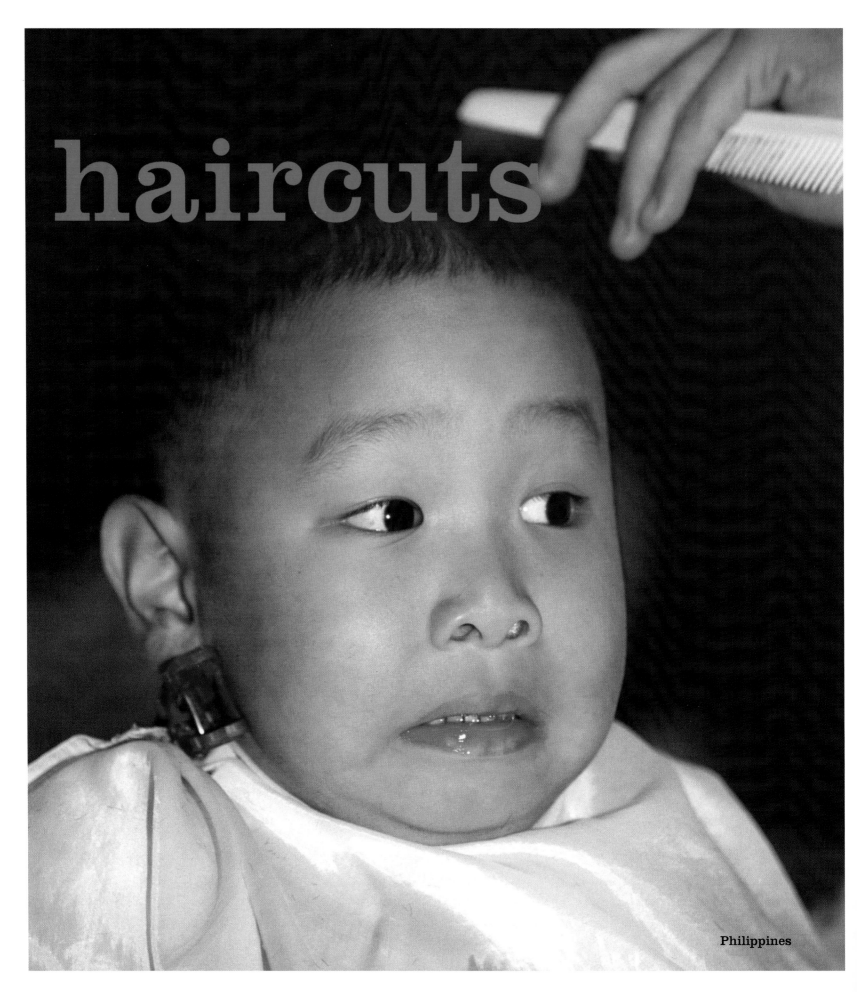

haircuts

Philippines

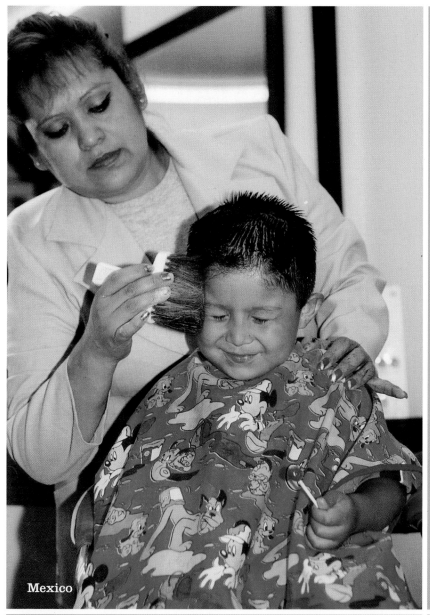

Mexico

My First (Bad) Haircut

I don't remember my first haircut, but I do remember a particularly bad one when I was six years old. My father didn't actually put a bowl over my head and cut around the edges, but that was the style he was going for. As soon as I saw myself in the mirror, I panicked. All I could think of was school the next day and how I would be teased by the other kids. My solution: a knit ski cap. The problem: I lived in Southern California, and by midmorning, it was hot and sunny. Recess was spent running from classmates who tried to grab the cap off my head. Somehow I eluded them, but by the time I returned to my desk, sweat was trickling down the side of my face and the cap was smooshed down almost over my eyes. That was when my teacher, Miss Garrells, finally persuaded me to remove it. It was actually a relief. I got teased of course, but I survived. And the hair grew back.

—Mark Teague

I 'member my first haircut.
I don't like haircuts. My neck
always itches after.

—Jenica, age 4, USA

Peru

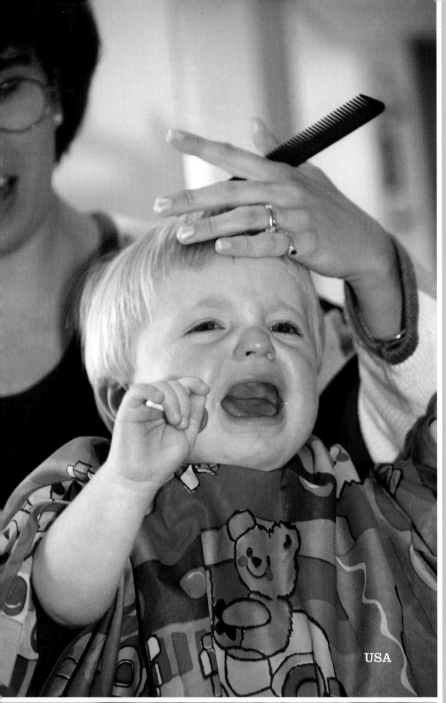

USA

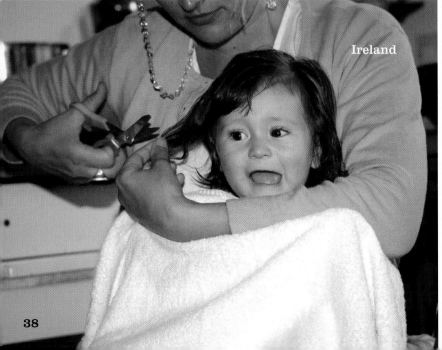

Ireland

Extreme Makeover

I stand outside Verna's Beauty Parlor in downtown Cedar Rapids, Iowa. Ten years old, I am about to have my first haircut. Pushing open the door, I breathe in the steamy ammonia-tinged air, vibrating with the roar of seven hair dryers hanging over a row of lavender-smocked ladies. Ruby nails gleaming, faces glowing, they leaf through the pages of *McCalls, Ladies Home Journal,* and *The Saturday Evening Post,* oblivious to my imminent initiation.

Suitably smocked, I study myself in the mirror, hating what I see: long red pigtails, pale freckled skin, huge brown eyes, and an irritating pug nose. Never mind. I am about to be transformed.

Verna stands behind me, kiss curls glued to her rouged cheeks. "You sure you want to do this?" she asks, hoisting my braids in one hand.

Barely able to contain my excitement, I nod. My stylish cut will be the envy of every girl in the fifth grade.

From a metal tray bristling with brushes, plastic curlers, bobby pins, and clips, Verna pulls out a pair of shears. Frowning, she tips my head back while I, feeling like Marie Antoinette, wait for the chop.

An hour later, hacked, permed, blow-dried, sprayed, and tweaked, I can't help but notice the horrified look on my mother's face as she surveys my close-cropped helmet of tight red curls. "It will grow," she says hopefully.

The boys call me Shirley Temple. The girls offer hair-straightening tips. I cry myself to sleep.

Two weeks later I am fitted with blue-framed eyeglasses, braces on my teeth, and a hideous metal headpiece that must be worn for sixteen hours every single day until I am in seventh grade.

Nothing was ever the same again.

—Kathy Eldon

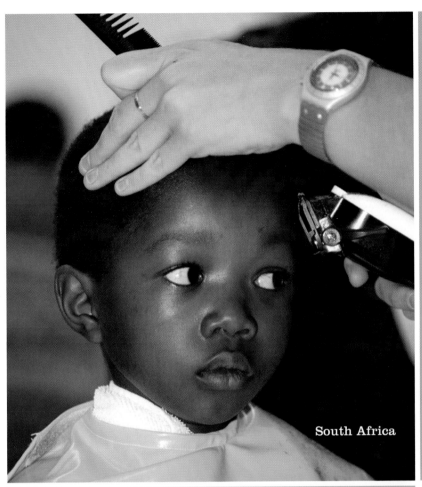

South Africa

Malaysia

I don't like for anybody to cut my hair, because it's creepy.

—Fernando, age 5, Venezuela

When I was 4 years old, I had never had a haircut and my mother combed my hair in a ponytail all the time—sometimes using a rubber band, and sometimes just in a braid. One day my father said that he would take me to get a haircut. I was glad because some kids used to tease and call me "girl." We went to the barber and he gave me a haircut.

—Clifton, age 9, Belize

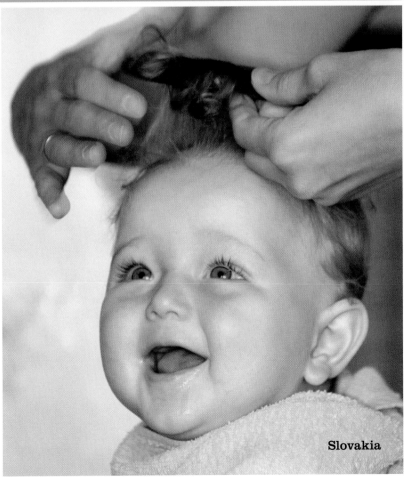

Slovakia

school

St. Lucia

On the first day of school I saw three kids, named Lyra Bengamin and Charlie. I went to them. I askt them there names and then Charlie tell jokes. Then Lyra showd us how well she could draw. Then we did a play. Charlie was an old women.

—Sherene, age 7, USA

My first day of school was good, because it has a music room.

—Fernando, age 5, Venezuela

My first day of school I was verry emberesed. I hold on to my mom and cried, momy stay, stay! My teacher was very nice. I went to first grad and now I'm in third grad and met a best frend. The end.

—Arturo, age 8, USA

Sri Lanka

First Day of School

When I think back to my first day of school, it is a dream I had the night before that stands out most clearly. In it, I was riding in a convertible with the top down, while my mother, looking as glamorous as a movie star, drove. I was standing on the seat next to her (remember, this was a dream), holding on to the windshield as I smiled into the wind that whipped back my hair. I felt incredibly strong and free.

In reality, I don't remember how I got to school that first morning, but I do remember clinging tearfully to my mother's legs as she introduced me to my kindergarten teacher and said, "Isn't it nice? Your teacher's name is the same as your brother's: Mrs. Lee." I didn't care what her name was. I just wanted to go home with my mother where I'd feel safe. I don't know how long I cried after my mother left, but I do remember that I felt anything but strong and free. I think it's interesting that although both the feelings in the dream and those in reality have stayed with me all these years, it is the dream that stands out. That early dream taught me a lesson that has stayed with me: We have courage we don't know we have, and conquering what scares us most will make us strong and set us free.

—**James Howe**

Philippines

I grew up in Zimbabwe in Africa, but, hey, the school I went to looked pretty much like any school around the world. The activities were much the same, the teachers were much the same, the lessons were much the same, and the sports were much the same, so it wasn't quite as exotic as it sounds.

I loved school. I was into everything except sports: debating, choir, drama productions, school magazines, and so on. I entered a public speaking competition run by the British Commonwealth Society.

I won! I was ecstatic. It was my undoing, really. I've been giving speeches ever since. I don't think I've stopped talking, either in public or in private, for the last forty years!

—**Mem Fox**

I remember when I went to my first day at the Humboldt School. I saw my friend Andres. I didn't know that he was going to my same school, and then I met Daniel the crazy, because he always says crazy things.

—Marco, age 4, Venezuela

USA

Peru

On Beginning School

When I was a little girl, I lived with my grandmother and grandfather in a small white house in Cool Ridge, West Virginia. It was very far out in the country, with mountains all around.

When I became old enough to go to school, I had to walk out the dirt road we lived on to catch the school bus. In the winter it was always dark when I left. And my grandfather put on his coat and watched me walk off into the dark morning. Sometimes there were other children to walk with. Sometimes not.

My grandfather stood at the fence and watched. At one point, the road dipped down a hill and I disappeared. He waited until he saw my small figure walking up the other side of the hill. He waited until he saw the lights of the school bus. He waited until I was safely on.

Then he went back inside to the warm kitchen, the coal-burning stove, the smell of lard biscuits and bacon, and to my grandmother, who had been with him such a long time and who was now raising yet another child who needed help finding a school bus in the dark.

—Cynthia Rylant

Mexico

On my first day of school I got sick
and I was going to throw up. I got real sick
when I had to go to Spanish class. Then I got
a drink of water and I was o.k. and I learned how
to talk Spanish—uno, dos, tres, cat-ro, seis,
owch-o, and something else kinda like dit'es.
And I talked to Shay and to Pearl and I didn't
know them but now they are my friends. And
Shay is like a snapping turtle cause she won't
let me open the door when I want to open
it first and she has to do it.

—Brooklyn, age 4, USA

Raffi, age 4

My First Day at the Armenian School in Cairo

My mother often told of how miserable I was on my first day of school. I was four years old, dressed in my new light-blue school uniform and carrying a big wicker lunch box, on the front of which was a brass plate with my name engraved in Armenian. When we arrived at Kalousdian School that fateful day, little Raffi was not going to go inside his classroom, no matter how hard Mama pulled and cajoled.

There I was in the hallway, unwilling to budge, while Mama conferred with Mrs. Aghavnie, the kindergarten teacher. Mrs. Aghavnie brought out a colorful toy and put it halfway between me and the classroom door, and as I slowly took a few steps toward it she drew it closer to the door, and this went on until I made my way into the classroom, more focused on the toy than the strange new world I had just entered.

—Raffi

When I was in second grade my parents asked that we walk two miles to school so we wouldn't be seen arriving in a car. Many of the other children's families didn't have cars, or lived closer to school so they could walk. There was no public school bus, and we lived in the country. We didn't want to appear to be different. As we passed a church, young kids started to throw stones at us. They were apparently of one religious faith and we were of another.

That grade school experience must have left a deep mark with me, for ever since I have been very busy trying to bring people together no matter their cultural, national, gender, or racial differences. That's what human rights are all about. When people don't know about your religion or race or anything else about you, they become afraid, and that can lead to hatred. Ignorance leads to fear leads to hate leads to violence.

And we not only need to learn more about each other, but we also need to learn how to prevent violence and how to make peace.

—Cora Weiss

I more

Sri Lanka

St. Lucia

My First Day at School

I had two first days of school because I started school in the United States, where I was born, and then again in Germany, when my family moved back to their country of origin when I was six years old. And my school experiences were not only far apart geographically; they were two very different experiences, both unforgettable for different reasons. In Syracuse, New York, I remember vividly the sun-filled room and large sheets of paper, colorful paints and brushes. I had a very kind teacher, Miss Frickey, who encouraged my parents to nurture their young son's creative interests. In Germany, the following year, I encountered corporal punishment. For a minor infraction, I received three strikes on both of my upward-facing palms with a bamboo stick. When I realized my family was not going to return to the States, I decided to become a bridge builder and build a bridge between the two countries and take my Oma, my grandmother, across the wide ocean.

—Eric Carle

doctors and dentists

Dr. Kyriazi is really fun. I always get a cool band aid and a sticker. He like to talk to my mom a lot and we always see him on Saturday morning after cartoons.

—Shelby, age 8, USA

The first time I saw the dentist I was 6 years old. And they took out a back tooth and I was afraid because it was the first time for me, but that's all I remember. Except my tooth was bad, and that's why they took it.

—Yoni, age 10, Guatemala

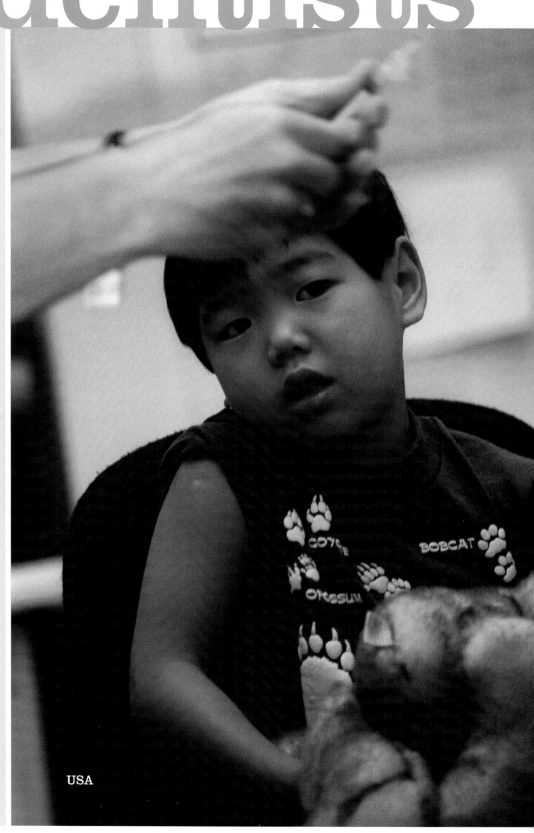

USA

Philippines

My great aunt Tillie was my dentist. She lived alone in a huge apartment on the Upper West Side of New York. Her office was a dark room in that apartment, full of dental torture instruments. But worse than that was her mustache. And her warts with bristly hair. And her wooden leg. We went to her house for dinner. She sprinkled colored cookie crumbs on the meat loaf. She limped and scraped carrying that meat loaf across the room. The dread with which I watched that meat loaf approach. I thought she must be some kind of witch. Or just plain nuts.

How could my parents allow her to work on my teeth? It was a mystery, as everything was when I was a child. Nothing was explained or discussed. Now I have straight teeth all lined up in a row. And Tillie is no longer on this earth. And now I think, well she was quite brave and smart. I miss the whole thing. Yes I do.

—**Maira Kalman**

When I went to the dentist in New York I was afraid to lay back on the chair! He took out two wigglies and then he cleaned all my teeth and then he gave me a tube of toothpaste and a little brush to take home!

—Isaiah, age 5, St. Lucia

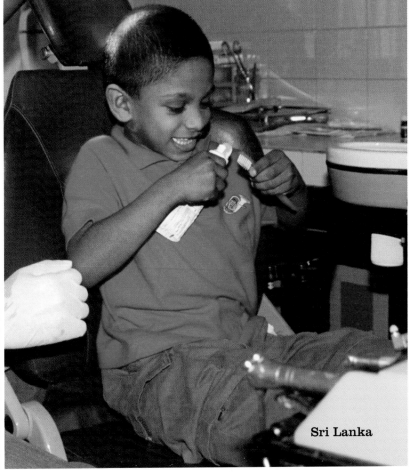

Sri Lanka

49

First Flight

Not long before my fourth birthday, my mother told me that I was going to go to Florida with her to visit her beloved Aunt Oodoo. ("Ruth" to relatives more prosaic than my mother.) I found the name of our destination enchanting, and the name of my unknown great aunt beyond perfect. Oodoo. Florida. Imagine.

Better yet, I'd be traveling by airplane, with my mother, without my three sisters, and it would be my birthday soon after we returned. How very wonderful to be almost four and everything so right.

Once on the airplane, encompassed by the fuzzy wool seat and elaborately safety-belted, I caught sight of an attractive, crisp, white thing, inserted in the pocket of the seat in front of me. My mother handed it to me, and I saw it was a little bag, and it bore the curious legend, "For Motion Discomfort." Motion Discomfort. This had an even lovelier cadence than Florida or Oodoo. (My own daughter, Darcy, has at age four this same open-mindedness about the sounds of words: For a time, she liked to call herself "Princess Glorious Mildew.")

My mother explained to me the function of the perky little bag, and this somehow only added to its allure. I secretly hoped, perhaps even resolved, that I would, sometime during the flight, experience the Motion Discomfort prerequisite to using the bag.

Mexico

And so I did. And my fever rose so high, and my shivering was so intense, and my mother was holding and holding me, and there were many other people who were moving around a lot, and I was being carried off the plane very fast, and my mother was always holding me, and then someone drove us to a much too bright room with doctors and nurses. Then suddenly we were back in Philadelphia, but not at my house. Instead we were at a place they said was the Children's Hospital, and there were lots of voices, and even though I very much didn't want them to, they put a lot of paste in my hair and then they put buttons with very long wires in the paste, but no one ever told me why, and my mother couldn't hold me all the time anymore because sometimes she had to go home to my sisters. There was a serious doctor named Dr. Button, probably named that because of all the buttons he kept putting in people's hair.

I had my fourth birthday in the hospital, and because April third was also the birthday of a boy there named Bruce—who was very old (seven) and very nice to me so I wished he could be my brother—we had two cakes: one yellow, and one half blue and half pink.

I don't know what the prevailing wisdom is about how one contracts encephalitis, but it's my opinion that it's because the airline people make those provocative little bags.

—**Sandra Boynton**

I had to get stitches becus my frend by axsidint hit me with a golf club. It hert a lot but I did it. I got stitches 2 times. The ferst time I got 5 stitches. The secont time I got 11 stichis.

—Benji, age 7, USA

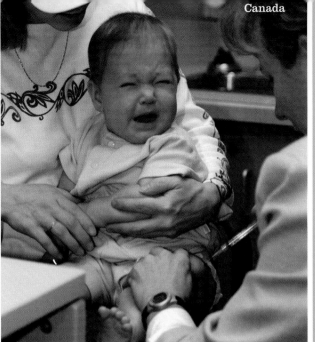
Canada

My mummy told me that she was taking me to the dentist. When I was in the chair, I thought he was going to take out my teeth! But he just cleaned them and I felt fine. My mummy says that I must go back again soon.

—Denise, age 5, St. Lucia

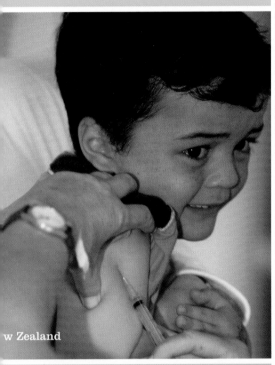
w Zealand

I don't like the doctor. Everything is always cold. The scale scares me because it moves funny and I always have to get shots.

—Daniel, age 5, USA

Ireland

I only went to the dentist one time when my tooth hurt. I was very scared, and the dentist had to pull it out because it wasn't a good one anymore. We didn't go there before. Now there is a hole and I can stick my tongue into it. It feels funny.

—Israel, age 10, Guatemala

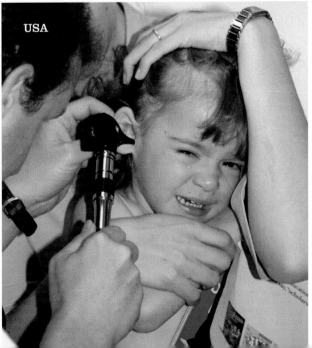
USA

I was afraid to go to the dentist and I cried in the car. When I went the dentist took out my shaky tooth and made me wash my mouth. She gave me a little toothpaste and a brush to take home.

—Jayda, age 5, St. Lucia

pets

Philippines

South Africa

My first pet was a lovable gray little kitten, which I named Fluffy. She was barely six weeks old when I got her. What I remember most about her was the first night that she slept with me. She was on my chest all night long licking my nose, when she wasn't sleeping. When I awoke the next morning and looked into the mirror of my mother's eyes, I had a truly rough and reddened little nose. I was five years old.

—**Synthia Saint James**

Mexico

USA

I'd always wanted a pet, but because the area we lived in was so small and restricted it was hard to choose a suitable pet. We couldn't get a dog or a cat but we did have a small pond in the garden so the ideal pet was a fish or something living under water. One of my parent's friends had a pond and they offered us an animal of our choice from their back garden. We arrived at their house and looked in the pond. Fishes and tadpoles swam around. Then something flew up into the air and landed near my foot. I stooped and picked it up and claimed that I wanted a frog as my pet. I named him "Freddie" and he was medium sized and smooth-skinned and I beamed with pride every time I saw him jumping and swimming in the water.

—Sam, age 12, United Kingdom

53

I woke up very excited on my eighth birthday. My brother accidentally spilled the beans the night before, telling me I was getting a loop-to-loop Hot Wheels set—the second item on my list. "Puppy" was at the top of my birthday list, but my parents said a dog was too much work for a boy.

After a special birthday lunch, Dad loaded us all in his Volkswagen bus to go to our little college town's Dairy Queen; a tradition for us with summer birthdays. Heading down Main Street, we drove right by the DQ (Dad had a habit of taking side errands when in town.) I just wanted my extra large chocolate-cherry dipped cone and my birthday present.

Dad headed toward the university, probably to pick up something on campus before we got ice cream. Then he passed by his office. I bounded to the front of the bus asking where we were going. He grinned widely toward my mom, ignoring me completely. I felt disappointed. It was my birthday after all. Dad's dumb errands…

He pulled up behind a small house where a lady met us in her backyard. Following behind was a tired, hot beagle, wagging her tail. Behind the mother beagle were five adorable little puppies. Dad looked at me and simply said, "Choose."

I whipped around, "What?"

"Choose which puppy you want. Happy Birthday!"

My stomach flip-flopped. Bending down, I was instantly mobbed by all five puppies, licking and biting at my ears, wrestling for my attention. The smallest, a tiny brown-and-white boy pup, crawled into my lap resting his face on my leg, one eye closed lazily and the other looking intently into mine, as if to say, "You are my boy now."

I kissed him on the nose, falling instantly in love. On the way home we got my new puppy a large bag of puppy chow. I named him Frisky.

I forgot all about the loop-to-loop Hot Wheels set—until Christmas, that is.

—Justin Matott

Philippines

Ecuador

My favorite pet is a cat. I love it so much that I hug it. One day it attack me. Then it said in cat language, I'm sorry. But then my cat wanted to eat and I sed yes. I want to play with my cat. I love it.

—Quetzalli, age 7, USA

When I got my first turtle that was my first birthday. I was one. His name is Rock cause he looks like one. He's getting too big awlready. Last winter we lef him outside when I was 5 and I forgot. He dug a hol and my frend found him. I was happy.

—Esai, age 7, USA

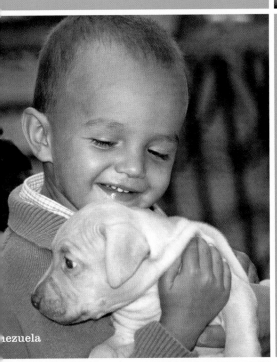

Even though we already had two dogs, they were in our family before I was born and I wanted a pet of my own. I wanted a puppy. One day my parents took me to see some puppies and they bought a rottweiler puppy just for me. They made me promise to take good care of it and to train it and be sure it didn't get into any trouble because it was now my responsibility. I named it Bruno.

—Sean, age 10, Belize

Canada

Sadie was our first dog. She was a Chihuahua and peed everywhere. Mom and Dad made us give her back. Then we got Ginger, she is great, half German Shepard and half Chow. She pees outside and she's my best friend.

—Luke, age 5, USA

Peru

One very moving moment of life was when my parents gave me a parakeet called Jazmin. I played with her and she even yawned!!! She played football and liked to wag from one side to the other on her ball and also in her cage. We had incredible moments with her.

—Cristina, age 8, Venezuela

55

Early Green Chores

Fresh and green in the summer heat, beans and peas from our garden to our supper plates. My job was the bridge. Pinching off both tips of each bean then snapping each bean in half. Tips in the blue bowl. Supper in the red. Fresh peas were a gift to open and share. Press and pop the pod package then scoop out the treasure with my learning thumb as the line of peas shot bouncing toward the bowl. Some in the bowl for mother to cook. A few right then for me to eat with a crunch as I tasted green.

—George Shannon

Ireland

When I was five, I learned to make my own bed. At school I learned about recycling rubbish, and I got to be head of recycling at home. Now I get to place the bin outside the gate every collection day.

—Liam, age 8, New Zealand

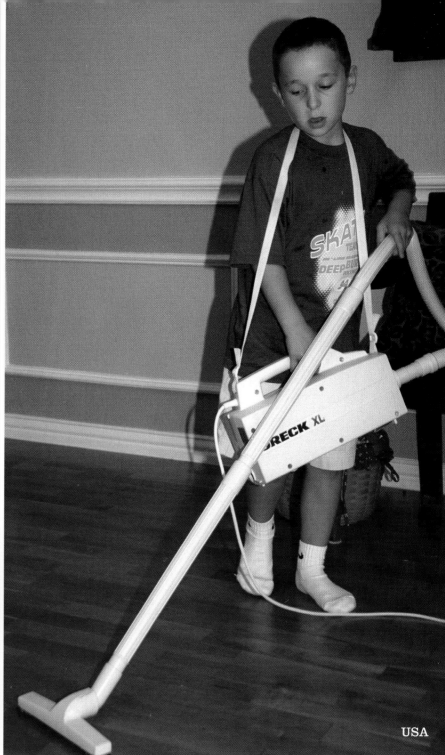

USA

Philippines

When you grow up in the country, as I did, chores often included such things as taking care of chickens, cows, rabbits, ducks, and even horses, as well as the indoor ones like hanging up clothes, dusting, and washing dishes. So doing chores was a big part of life, and you either learned to cope or went around being miserable.

I coped by turning my chores into games. My game for doing the dishes (my most hated chore) was that I was a poor, mistreated slave and my mother was the cruel slavemaster, and if I didn't get a certain amount done before she came in to check on me, I would be beaten and thrown in the dungeon. Of course we didn't really have a dungeon, and I was never beaten, but I was able to pretend well enough to make a boring chore rather exciting.

I had other exciting games for lots of other chores. For instance, when I had to gather eggs I was Jack in the Beanstalk gathering golden eggs from under the giant's geese—and the evil giant was watching me!!!

—Zilpha Keatley Snyder

Slovakia

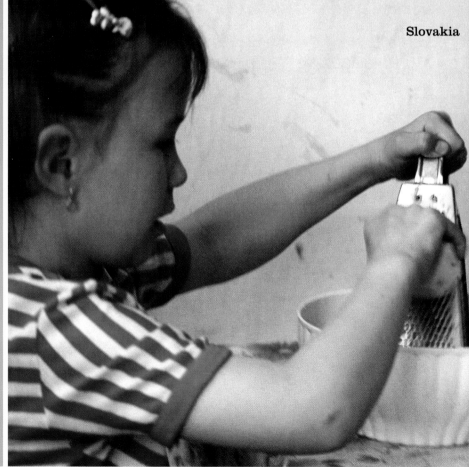
Slovakia

When I was growing up, my mom was in a wheelchair from polio and couldn't move her arms or legs. That never stopped her. When it was time to fix dinner, she would read from a cookbook, and all four kids would career around the kitchen with various tasks. She would instruct, "Get a cup of flour." My younger sister would dip the measuring cup in the bag of flour and lurch toward the bowl, spilling flour on everything. I'd tell her to scrape the excess off with a knife. She'd yell back that it was fine like it was. Mom would be saying above the din, "You have to be exact with flour." Meanwhile, my baby brother would be hacking at a tomato with a fork because we wouldn't let him touch the knives. Somehow dinner got on the table. We even had dinner parties! We made wild things, at least compared to what was usually cooked in our little farming community. Welsh rabbit, chutney, and mole came out of our kitchen. The kids tried to take credit for the good cooking in our family because we did the hands-on work. Dad always gave Mom the credit because she was the idea person. We implemented her vision of family, meal by meal.

—**Barbara O'Brien**

USA

South Africa

glasses

USA

India

It all started in 2nd grade! Now back then glasses were really cool to have or that is what all my friends and I thought. So the day my best friend Alexis came into class in glasses, I turned green with jealousy. I begged my mom to get me some but then she explained that you only get glasses if you have bad eyesight. Right then my hopes faded away. But then miraculously a couple of months later my teacher told my mom that I had been squinting a lot in class and that I needed my eyes checked. "Yes!" I thought. The next thing I knew I was at the eye doctor getting my eyes examined. After all these tests I was told I would need a pair of glasses. I got to look around and pick out whatever pair I wanted. I finally decided on a round-framed pair. I thought it was the best thing that ever happened to me. So I got my glasses and I walked out of the store with my mom feeling totally cool and confident. Then my brother looked at me and yelled 'four eyes' and I cried.

—Taylor, age 13, USA

Ireland

New Zealand

Malaysia

I remember getting my first pair of glasses at the age of eight. I desperately wanted them. I thought they would add interest and distinction to a nondescript, round, freckly face. What was more, one of my best friends had just started wearing glasses, and somehow she made them seem very glamorous; I especially liked the little hard case she had for them, with a silk square for wiping the lenses. So I told my mother, quite truthfully as it happened, that I couldn't see anything the teacher wrote on the blackboard unless I sat right at the front of the class, and in due course she took me off to the optician's, where he loaded the bridge of my nose with a heavy contraption that could hold several removable lenses at a time. "Better, worse, or the same?" he asked me, turning what looked like miniature magnifying glasses in front of each eye as I tried to identify blurry black letters on a hazy white board. I gave my answers nervously—was I doing too well, would he send me away spectacle-less? Finally he lifted the heavy weight off my face and announced that, yes, I was very shortsighted.

The thrill of it—I had passed! The excitement of choosing between the free blue, pink, or tortoiseshell plastic frames! Getting my own hard little case and silk wiper! And the completely unexpected, wondrous miracle that happened a week later, when I wore my glasses home and was able to see individual blades of grass at my feet as we walked through the park and the faces of drivers in passing cars as we turned into our street and the number on our front door when we were still five houses away!

And the awful fall my pride took when the very first little boy called me "four-eyes" at school next day.

—J. K. Rowling

USA

Malaysia

St. Lucia

biographical information

Sandra Boynton has written and illustrated forty books since 1979, including *The Going to Bed Book, Dinos to Go,* and *Moo, Baa, La La La!* She lives and works chaotically with her family in the Berkshire Hills, USA. Her most recent children's book/CD, *Philadelphia Chickens,* was nominated for a Grammy award.

Eric Carle is the acclaimed illustrator and author of more than seventy brilliantly illustrated and innovatively designed picturebooks for very young children. His best-known work, *The Very Hungry Caterpillar,* has eaten its way into the hearts of children all over the world and has been translated into more than thirty languages and sold over eighteen million copies.

Joy Cowley began to write for children as a way to help her son with his reading. Since then, she has written more than 400 books for early readers, including *Mrs. Wishy-Washy, The Rusty, Trusty Tractor,* and *Big Moon Tortilla.* She was born in New Zealand, where she lives today with her husband and their animals on a farm by the sea.

Kathy Eldon has worked as an art teacher, television presenter, magazine editor, journalist, media consultant, and a television and film producer in Kenya, England, and the United States. In 1999, she executive produced a CNN documentary about the Colombian children's peace movement, nominated for the Nobel Peace Prize. Kathy and her daughter, Amy, are the founders of the Creative Visions Foundation, which helps fund young writers, journalists, and photographers produce commercial projects with a social, humanitarian, or environmental focus.

Mem Fox has written dozens of children's books, including *Possum Magic,* the best-selling children's book in Australia (two million copies sold!). For twenty-four years she was associate professor, literacy studies, in the School of Education at Flinders University, South Australia, and now works as an international literacy consultant.

Katharine Holabird is the joint creator, with Helen Craig, of the enduringly popular *Angelina Ballerina* books, which have been translated into six languages and received the Kentucky Bluegrass Award, the British Book Design and Production Award, and the Child Study Association's Children's Book of the Year for 1990.

James Howe has written novels, nonfiction, adaptations of classic stories, screenplays for movies and television, and lots and lots of picturebooks, including *Bunnicula, Horace and Morris, but Mostly Dolores, There's a Dragon in My Sleeping Bag,* and the *Sebastian Barth Mysteries.*

William Joyce is the author and illustrator of many books, such as *Santa Calls, The Leaf Men and the Brave Good Bugs, Dinosaur Bob and his Adventures with the Family Lazardo,* and *Bentley and Egg.* His illustrations have also graced many covers of *The New Yorker.* Two of his books, *George Shrinks* and *Rolie Polie Olie,* have been adapted as animated TV series, and *Buddy* was made into a live-action film. He even created pre-production art for *Toy Story.*

Maira Kalman is the author-illustrator of several groundbreaking, fantastical, lyrical children's books, including the celebrated series about Max Stravinsky, the poet dog. Her artwork frequently appears on the cover of *The New Yorker,* and she is a regular contributor to *The New York Times* and *Atlantic Monthly.* Maira also runs M&Co, a multidisciplinary design studio.

Margaret Mahy is a New Zealand native who worked as a librarian and writer-in-residence until 1980, when she became a full-time writer, specializing in children's books. She won the Esther Glen Medal of the New Zealand Library Association for *The Haunting* and has been awarded the Carnegie Medal of the British Library Association three times for *The Haunting, The Changeover: A Supernatural Romance,* and *The Memory.*

Justin Matott is an author of many children's books, including *Oliver Kringle,* as well as several books for grown-up children. He writes book reviews for the *Rocky Mountain News* and spends much of his time inspiring young writers in schools all over the country. He lives in Colorado with his wife, two sons, his dogs Snickers and Tootsie Roll, and his cat, Baby Ruth.

Kara May, the author of many books for young people including *Joe Lion's Big Boots, The Dream Snatcher,* and *Yeti Boy,* worked as a radio actor as a child in Australia. Kara lives in London, where she works as a part-time teacher in fiction at Goldsmith's College and writes plays as well as books.

Megan McDonald, author of the award-winning *Judy Moody* books, says, "Sometimes I think I *am* Judy Moody." The author grew up as the youngest of five sisters in Pittsburgh, Pennsylvania. Megan has since written twenty-five books for children and also made a living as a storyteller and a park ranger. She lives with her husband in Sebastopol, California.

Oscar Misle is the director and founder of CECODAP, a grassroots organization that works on the promotion and defense of children's rights in Venezuela.

Daniel Möller is the author of the hip-hop kids', stories *Word to Your Mother!* and *Du! Hitta rytmen,* which won a Swedish Debutante Prize and was nominated for best children's book in 2001. He is a native of Sweden.

Marisa Montes sees herself as a children's book author, artist, lawyer, legal writer and editor, humorist, motivational speaker, linguist, feminist, disabled-person's-rights and Affirmative Action advocate all rolled into one. She has written many books, including *Juan Bobo Goes to Work* and *Egg-Napped.*

Naomi Shihab Nye has written many books, including National Book Award finalist *19 Varieties of Gazelle: Poems of the Middle East* and *Habibi,* a novel for teens that won six Best Book awards. She has also been a Guggenheim Fellow, a Library of Congress Witter Bynner Fellow, and a Lannan Fellow.

Barbara O'Brien is a children's advocate and president of the Colorado Children's Campaign.

Stephen Pankhurst is the founder of FriendsReunited.com in the United Kingdom, an internet-based personal search engine that enables schoolmates and others to reestablish lost relationships.

Raffi is an internationally acclaimed family entertainer, songwriter, author, and ecology advocate. Since 1974, he has charted a unique career with unprecedented success, including hundreds of sold-out performances in North America's premier theaters and sales of millions of gold and platinum albums, concert videos, and children's books. He recently served as honorary chair of UNEP's International Children's Conference on the Environment in Victoria, BC, and, with such classic songs as "Baby Beluga" and "Bananaphone," he has provided positive musical messages to generations of fans.

J. K. Rowling, author of the *Harry Potter* series, has won the Hugo Award, the Bram Stoker Award, and the Whitbread Award for Best Children's Book. She has also received special commendation for the Anne Spencer Lindbergh Prize, and a special certificate for being a three-year winner of the Smarties Prize, as well as many other honors. She has even been named an Officer of the British Empire.

Cynthia Rylant is a Newbery Medalist who published her first children's book in 1982. Since then she has written more than sixty books, including stories about favorite characters Poppleton, Mr. Putter and Tabby, and Henry and Mudge.

Synthia Saint James is a self-taught artist and author who has published thirteen picturebooks, three of which she wrote. She has received both a Coretta Scott King Honor and a Parents Choice Silver Honor.

Daniel San Souci is an award-winning author/illustrator of fifty books for children. Over the years his main focus has been wildlife. He is also the creator of the "Clubhouse Book Series" featuring a young Dan, who teams up with his brother (author Robert San Souci) on many fun and mischievous adventures.

George Shannon is the author of many books for young people, including three "Stories to Solve" books, *April's Showers, Lizard's Song,* and *Dance Away.* He spent years as a children's librarian and, later, a professional storyteller.

Zilpha Keatley Snyder has been writing books for children since 1964. The recipient of three Newbery Honor Book awards for *The Egypt Game, The Headless Cupid,* and *The Witches of Worm,* she has completed forty books.

Mark Teague worked in a bookstore after college, where he was inspired to begin his grown-up career as a writer and illustrator of children's books, including *How Do Dinosaurs Say Goodnight?, Dear Mrs. LaRue, Pigsty,* and *How I Spent My Summer Vacation.*

Uzo Unobagha was born in Nigeria and came to the United States in 1995. Her first book published in the U.S., *Off to the Sweet Shores of Africa and Other Talking Drum Rhymes,* was named an American Library Association Notable Book. She is also the multicultural and career specialist teacher at Thomas Jefferson Elementary School in Utica, New York.

Cora Weiss is president of the Hague Appeal for Peace and a Nobel Peace Prize nominee.

Pledge

- ☀ I pledge to notice the ways people are like me before I notice the ways they are different;

- ☀ I pledge to say only kind things to others and to stop myself before I say mean things;

- ☀ I pledge to use respectful words to work out my problems with other people;

- ☀ I pledge to encourage my friends to do these things too,

because . . .

I know that if everyone does these four things we will put an end to intolerance and hatred all over the world.